Captured, Frozen, Starved
—AND LUCKY

How One Jewish American GI Survived a Nazi Stalag

Milton Feldman

Feldman, Milton
Bauer, Seth
Captured, Frozen, Starved—and Lucky:
How one Jewish American GI Survived a Nazi Prison Camp

ISBN-13: 978-1-9865-0425-6
ISBN-10: 19865-0425-5

Book design by Joe Fierst

Photographs from public archives, Milton Feldman personal collection,
and © Eduardo Montes-Bradley

DEDICATION

I dedicate this book to my loving parents and family and to the four dear
friends who not only shared my time in prison camp,
but who also shared whatever it took to keep ourselves alive:
Blue Caldwell, Jimmy McCormick,
Joe Prinzinger, and Ben ter Beek.

PREFACE

The 106th Division, 423rd Infantry Regiment in the Battle of the Bulge

By Carl Wouters

Excerpted from http://106thinfantry.webs.com/historyofthe106th.html

I n December, 1944, the 106th Golden Lion Division relieved the 2nd Infantry Division in the Schnee Eifel sector of eastern Belgium and just across the German border. This area had been recaptured in September 1944. The terrain consisted of densely wooded hills and open rolling terrain, intercut with steep valleys. The GIs of the 106th were ordered to take over the 2nd Infantry's positions on a 'man for man, gun for gun' basis. The veterans of the 2nd assured them that this was the 'Ghost Front', and that they would have an easy life in the area ...

The German Fifth Panzer Army launched its assault against the 'Ghost Front' on the morning of 16 December, 1944. The battle that ensued would become known as the Battle of the Bulge.

In the week prior to the German breakthrough, the men of the 106th had observed enemy troop movements and heard the sounds of tanks, trucks and heavy equipment being assembled behind the German lines. This information was sent up to higher echelons but it was discarded as they believed that the Germans were tricking the newly arrived Americans. This sense of complacency ultimately led to the largest loss of materiel and manpower experienced on the Western Front.

On the morning of the 16th, thousands of German artillery pieces and rocket launchers opened up and heavily shelled the U.S. lines. Soon thereafter German troops of the 18th and 62nd Volksgrenadier Divisions began their assault on the positions of the 106th Division. The 14th Cavalry Group in the Losheim Gap was overrun by German armored and paratroop units. Their withdrawal to the Belgian border exposed the left flank of the 422nd Infantry. Another German breakthrough in Bleialf on the morning of the 17th allowed for a German pincer movement, which trapped the 422nd and 423rd Infantry Regiments on the Schnee Eifel.

A promised counterattack and an air drop with supplies to the besieged 422nd and 423rd Infantry Regiments never happened. By December 18, 1944, the two units—still holding their original positions despite being surrounded—were ordered to reverse direction, break through the German attack and reconnect with the American forces. A cross-country march brought the 423rd Infantry to the outskirts of Schönberg, where a final attack on the morning of 19 December

1944 led to many casualties. Out of ammunition, water, food and medical supplies, the remnants of the Regiment were surrendered by Colonel Charles C. Cavender. An hour later, some five miles north of them, Colonel George L. Descheneaux Jr. of the 422nd Infantry Regiment reached the same conclusion. Approximately 8,000 men became prisoners of war.

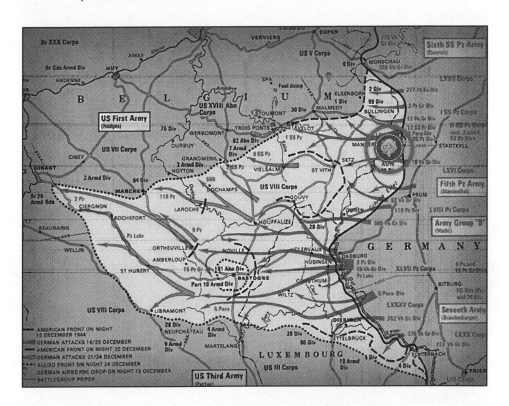

CHAPTER

— ONE —

I'm a veteran of WWII, a Jewish American soldier who was captured during the Battle of the Bulge and held in a Nazi prison camp until the Russians liberated it just weeks before the end of the war. Not far away, the members of my family who had not emigrated to the U.S.— aunts, uncles, cousins, grandparents—had been brought to other camps for slavery and slaughter.

My story is unusual in that there were relatively few Jewish GIs in German prison camps. But my war was also in many ways entirely common. Nearly all capable men of my generation served in the military during the war. Like the vast majority, I wasn't designing strategy or committing thousands to battle; I was just there to do whatever they asked of me as a private in the infantry. Every soldier in every theater of war had individual moments of bravery, bonding, despair, fear, anger, and deprivation. Millions were killed or maimed; those of us who were not were just lucky. We all were exposed to the horror of mass warfare and its impact not only on the soldiers on both sides but on families, on societies, on the cities and towns and farms that people had carefully constructed over centuries, on our collective systems for food and trade and health care. On the ways we treat other human beings. In short, on human civilization.

As a result, I am very anti-war. I thought the saying that war is hell was obvious, but apparently, it's not, because wars still happen. In war, everyone loses. The only positive thing about war is the rebuilding of civilization that follows, a reminder that humans can be constructive, cooperative, and prosperous. In my later years, I loved traveling to Europe with my wife, Shirley, to see its rebirth and the healthy societies that replaced a murderous ideology and decades of destruction and misery.

As I write this, I just celebrated my 94th birthday. I'm doing this primarily for my family, but also for anyone who might be interested. As time passes, it becomes harder for people to grasp what World War II was like on a global scale, with tens or hundreds of millions involved in the conflict. At the same time, if people don't hear individual stories like mine, they might never imagine what it's like to have one shriveled apple and the small act of kindness it represented offer a brief glimmer of hope for survival and recovery at a moment of utter despair. Or think about being 19 years old, having surrendered your weapon and your dignity to the Germans, and under pressure to declare your religion in a Nazi prison camp.

Recently, I celebrated the birth of my great grandson, Elliot Feldman. He will be too young to hear my story directly from me. I hope this book opens his—and all readers'—eyes to both the misery of war and the humanity of shared experience.

CHAPTER

— TWO —

My parents were both immigrants, part of the massive migration of Russian and Polish Jews to the U.S. at the turn of the 20th century. In 1897, Russia was home to more than 5 million Jewish people, about half of the global population of Jews. By law, nearly all of them lived in a region called the Pale of Settlement, a swath cut across the 25 westernmost Russian provinces. Russia was industrializing, and like many countries at that time, its rule by aristocracy was increasingly shaky. The changing economy led to economic deprivation and, in turn, to the oppression of Russian Jews. Beginning in the 1880s, the Russians instituted laws limiting Jewish commercial activity and booting Jews out of major cities, including Moscow. Russian soldiers killed thousands of their fellow citizens in pogroms, vicious raids on the villages where Jews were permitted to live. Between 1881 and 1914, 1.5 million Jewish immigrants left Russia for the U.S., many in dire circumstances.

My mother, Bessie Lucas, came here from Kiev in 1910. She was four years old. Her father, Max (Mannas Lukasz), had come to America in 1907 and when he could, he sent for the rest of the family: my grandmother, Fannie, my mother's older sister, Celia, my mother, and her younger brother, Jimmy. They sailed on the Ryndam from Rotterdam in November. Family immigration gets denigrated as "chain migration" now, presented as an insidious invasion, but nearly all immigrants throughout American history were part of extended families that reunited here. I'm convinced that the social and financial support of the brothers, sisters, aunts and uncles who came to the U.S. allowed the succeeding generations to become successful Americans.

My mother's family settled in a zinc mining town, Palmerton, Pennsylvania. The miners were primarily Hungarian immigrants, and I used to tease my mother that when she first learned English, she must have had a Hungarian accent.

I don't know a lot about her childhood in Palmerton (and later, Allentown), but I do know that she went to work in a shoe factory at the end of 8th grade, when she was about 14. Child labor laws and universal public education were relatively new then. You were allowed to work at that age as long as you attended a "continuation school" until you were 16. That's when her formal education ended.

My mother worked in the factory alongside my aunt. She was very smart—she was always an avid reader—and it must have shown. The man running the factory took her off the factory floor and trained her to be a shipping clerk. I don't know if she made any more money, but she worked at a desk. She remembered his support for her. Among other things he would occasionally ask, "What's your father's shoe size?" She'd tell him and he'd say, "Ah, this is a reject pair, just that size. Take it home." She got free shoes for the family.

My mother was very, very solid. She had to be self-educated and hard-working, and she was.

My father, Jack Feldman, was born in Rutka, a village in an area of the Pale that was passed back and forth between Russian and Poland, in 1892. He left, probably around 1910, in part to avoid serving in the Russian Army. He was likely to be drafted, and that army was not a good place for a young Jewish man. He didn't tell many stories about his exit, but I can imagine it. Apparently, he walked all the way across Europe over many months. Eventually he got to Belgium, where he learned to be a diamond cutter.

He got to America around 1914, just in time to serve in the U.S. Army in World War I (the U.S. joined the battle in 1917). Though I suspect he still spoke English poorly when he joined up, later on, nobody knew that my father was not born in this country. I figure that he lost his accent in the Army. My father was proud to be an American, and proud of his service. He was in the American Legion, and he almost always got to carry the flag in parades. I still have his helmet and other memorabilia, now more than 100 years old.

My father was in the 2nd Division, one of the prime divisions in the

Army. Serving his new country, he may have been in less danger from his fellow soldiers than he would have been in the Russian Army, but my father was immensely lucky to return from the war safely. He fought in most of the major battles that the U.S. Army was part of: Belleau Wood, Chateau-Thierry, the Second Battle of the Marne, San Michel. In just one of the battles, the division suffered 8,200 casualties.

Twenty-five years later, when I went into battle, my Division, the 106th, was assigned to relieve a division that had been fighting all through France: the 2nd Division. Until recently, I had not realized the coincidence: I was in the last division to be formed in WWII, and we replaced my father's division.

Shortly after my parents married, my father bought a store at 791 Onderdonk Avenue in the Ridgewood section of Queens, New York. It was a mostly German neighborhood then. The store had three rooms in back, and we lived there for several years after I was born until we could afford an apartment.

The store was known as a candy store, but now we'd call it a convenience store. It had an ice cream fountain with six revolving seats. They sold newspapers, candy, tobacco, and other things. It was a small store, but they made a living, even during the Depression.

My two parents ran the store without any help. It was an enormous challenge. Trading shifts, they kept the store open 18 hours a day. People then commonly bought several newspapers throughout the day. Newspapers had a morning edition, an afternoon edition, and then the "bulldog" edition which came at midnight, supposedly for sale early in the morning. It was that paper, though, that made my parents keep the store open at night. The bulldog edition had the day's horse racing results. The local numbers game—an illegal lottery—pegged its winners to the results at the track. People playing the numbers wanted to buy the paper at midnight to see if they'd won. It meant that my parents were operating the store from early morning until after midnight.

In the 1930s, there were people from many places living in Queens. The store carried at least half a dozen foreign or foreign-language newspapers: The Statszeitung was the German paper; The Irish Echo; Il Progresso was in Italian; The Forward was in Yiddish.

I was a sickly kid. I had rheumatic fever when I was about three years old, and the doctor said he was going to quarantine the family—which meant closing the store. My father said, "If you do that, I'm going to go bankrupt." So, the doctor, who was from my father's town in Poland, made a deal with him. My father stayed in the store, my mother stayed in the apartment with me, and they did not see each other until I recovered.

My mother was allowed to open the door to pass my father food, but that was all. The store stayed open.

When I was six years old, in 1930, my brother, Arthur Lewis Feldman, was born, which was great. I liked him.

Arthur was fine for about a year and a half, and then he contracted childhood leukemia. The average life expectancy of an American boy born in 1930 was only 58 years, and a big reason for the low average was that many people did not survive childhood. So many diseases were not preventable or treatable then. Arthur only lived another year or so, then he passed away. I was very aware of being Arthur's older brother, even after he'd died. People who later thought I was an only child were wrong: I had a brother.

I also had uncles. My mother had four younger brothers, stretched out about four years apart, and the youngest, Leo, was only seven years older than I. I was almost like a fifth brother. Several of them came to live with us at various times, and they always treated me as a brother. They would take me to baseball games—we went to the Brooklyn Dodgers' first night game, among many others. I remember sitting in the upper stands, and the lighting wasn't very good yet—a fly ball would disappear, and the outfielder had to wait until it got low enough to see. As an experiment, they played with yellow baseballs. I was close to my uncles my entire life.

When my brother got sick, it was a real problem for my parents. My mother was very involved with him, and she couldn't be in the store. My father was almost running it himself.

That summer they sent me to sleep-away camp. I'm sure it was just to get me out of the house. I remember that my father came to visit me at camp and he arrived during rest time. I must have been very happy about it, because I can still see him coming up the stairs.

My first-grade teacher at P.S. 93 in Ridgewood was Mrs. McNarry, an old biddy, or at least that's how I saw her (she may have been half the age I am now). I had a crush on a little girl, Lois Bartell. She was a little blonde. I never even talked to her. When I came back the next year expecting to see her, she had moved away. That was the end of my first love affair.

When I was in 5th grade, there was a city-wide essay competition. I wrote an essay about how my brother's illness made me want to become a doctor. My essay didn't win in my classroom, but my mother really liked it, and she went to the teachers, who agreed to submit it to the next round. It won and I moved on in the competition. I didn't win the whole thing, but I remember that I was becoming known for that essay and that my mother had been proud enough to go to the school to fight to get it considered. That was not common then.

In the 8th grade, when I was about to graduate from P.S. 93, I took the entrance exam for an elite high school for boys in Manhattan: Townsend Harris, which had been created in the mid-1800s to prepare students for City College. It was then (and is again now) the top public high school in New York City. They admitted just 250 boys per year from the entire city of New York.

I was accepted. I used to say I was probably number 250, because the kids there were so smart. Jonas Salk had gone there just a few years earlier—and graduated when he was 15. Herman Wouk, Ira Gershwin, and Richard Rogers were all Townsend Harris graduates.

So, in the fall of 1938, I started high school, taking the subway every day from Queens to East 23rd Street in Manhattan.

As Hitler gained power in the 1930s, my neighborhood began to change. The population was largely composed of German immigrants, and as Germany began to seem more powerful and successful in the world, many German Americans became Nazi supporters. Right up until the U.S. entered the war in 1941, there were German American children attending Nazi camps in the summertime, and adults, members of the German American Bund, would put on swastikas and march in the streets of New York. One famous Bund rally, in Madison Square Garden in 1939, attracted more than 20,000 American Nazis.

I only remember one personal instance of anti-Semitism: I was invited over to a friend's house to play. He took out his toy soldiers and they were arm-banded Nazi figures. I told him I was Jewish, and his reaction was, "Jews have no God." I went home in tears.

My parents must have faced much more serious anti-Semitism, but they did not talk about it in front of me. For that matter, I don't remember hearing them talk much about the Depression or the New Deal. All I knew was that in 1938, my father said he had decided to sell the store and leave the neighborhood. We briefly moved to Brooklyn, near my grandparents. Six months after that, my father and his brother bought a bigger store in Larchmont, New York, and we moved to Westchester County.

Though we'd moved, I continued going to school in Manhattan. At 14, I had to commute alone with all the big shots from Wall Street on the New York, New Haven, and Hartford Railroad. My parents gave me carfare for the subway from the train to the school, which was on 23rd Street, 19 blocks from Grand Central Terminal. Carfare was five cents each way, but I cheated. I would walk the mile down from 42nd to 23rd Street in the morning to save a nickel, and walk back, if I could, in the afternoon. Then I'd have pocket money.

This was New York in 1938. The Empire State Building was less than 10 years old, by far the tallest building in the world, and it dwarfed the rest of Manhattan. Ella Fitzgerald, Benny Goodman, and The Andrews Sisters had the big music hits—and one of them, "Bei Mir Bist Du Schoen," was in Yiddish, thanks to Jewish songwriters and musicians. Joe DiMaggio had followed Babe Ruth and Lou Gehrig in leading the Yankees to the World Series title, which was of no use to me, a passionate Brooklyn Dodgers fan. Every day I got to be part of that amazing uproar, navigating Manhattan by myself. Tied to the store, my parents rarely went into the city.

One thing I did in Manhattan was pick up sheet music for sale in the store. My parents didn't know anything about music, and I knew what kids were listening to, so I would set up the order, then go to Tin Pan Alley—it was an actual building—pick up the order and bring it home on the commuter train.

One day I was in the store helping out, and a customer was thumbing through the sheet music. He went over to my mother behind the counter and said, "Mrs. Feldman, thank you for putting my song out there." And my mother said, "Oh, I know nothing about music. My son's over there if you want to talk to him." He walked over and said, "I understand you take care of the sheet music." I said, "Yes." He said, "Well that's my song." I looked at it, and the song was, "You Go to My Head." On the cover was a picture of Bing Crosby. I said, "You're not Bing Crosby." He said, "No, no, no, no, no." He pointed: "There." There was his name, John Frederick Coots, songwriter. Coots was quite famous. He published something like 700 songs, including "Santa Claus is Coming to Town."

Another time I was in the store, reading a magazine—probably a sports magazine. A man came in and began flipping through magazines right next to me. He picked out a couple and went over to the counter. When he reached for his wallet, he didn't have it. Again, my mother was behind the counter. He said, "Mrs. Feldman, I forgot my wallet. Would you trust me for these magazines?" Maybe it came to 50 cents.

My mother said, "Of course I will." He asked for a pad, scribbled something on it, and handed it to her. He said, "Give this to your son. It's good for two tickets to Yankee Stadium." The customer was Ed Barrow, the president of the Yankees.

But I was a Brooklyn Dodgers fan. I was going to have to swallow my pride to take advantage of Mr. Barrow's offer. Luckily, there was a salesman who used to come into the store. He was a young guy, in his early 20s, and we'd talk sports. He was a Yankee fan, I was a Dodger fan, and we would spar over it. When I told him Mr. Barrow had offered me tickets, he made me a deal: enough money to buy Dodgers tickets— including the train fare—in exchange for Mr. Barrow's Yankees tickets. Thanks to Ed Barrow of the Yankees, I got to see the Dodgers.

I was at Townsend Harris for the rest of the school year, but the commute was very difficult. The next year, I went to Mamaroneck High School.

When Pearl Harbor was attacked on December 7, 1941, the day that President Roosevelt said "would live in infamy," I was a 17-year-old senior in high school. I don't remember the feeling of the day, but I do remember that, while we listened to the news on the radio, the announcers called high-ranking military officers by name to report to duty. One of my mother's brothers, my Uncle Dave, had already served a tour in the Army. He wasn't a high-ranking officer, but he knew on that first day he'd be called back to serve. I watched as he went to the closet and pulled out his uniform.

Three of my uncles went into the Army right after Pearl Harbor. By the time I entered the Army in 1943, Dave had already been in two or three landings on the Pacific. He was my hero. I think now about my mother, with three brothers and her only son all serving in the deadliest war ever. Talk about bravery.

When I graduated high school in 1942, I had just turned 18. I knew that I would end up serving in the armed forces soon, but they were still offering student deferments then, so I entered Penn State right away, with the summer semester that began in June, 1942. Months later, a recruiting officer came to the campus and said that if we signed up for the Enlisted Reserve Corps, we'd be able to finish our educations "if possible." I wanted to stay in school as long as I could before I was called up. So, I volunteered for the Army, but I did it hoping to finish my college education. I didn't leave school and enlist as many other soldiers did.

Though I was only there for two semesters, I guess I worked pretty quickly, at least on one front. I had joined a Jewish fraternity, and one weekend we arranged to attend a semi-formal dance with the members of a Jewish sorority. Some of the guys in my fraternity were dating girls from the sorority, so they had dates, but for the rest of us, they just matched us up by height to escort the girls to the dance. I was paired with a Shirley Levine. When I saw her, I couldn't believe my good fortune.

You would have to be pretty lucky to find a perfect match that way—and we were. Shirley and I started seeing each other regularly, and soon I gave her my fraternity pin, which was a prelude to becoming engaged. We were 18 years old.

Of course, it wasn't possible to finish my education. The military needed everyone they could get. Between the end of 1941 and the war's end in the spring of 1945, more than 16 million Americans served in the United States Armed Forces.

Just six months later, at the end of the fall semester of 1942, they called up the reserves, and I was in the Army. I was ordered to report to Camp Upton on Long Island for induction.

CHAPTER

— THREE —

O ur commanding officer was Corporal Benny. I never knew his last name. Corporal Benny marched us to a supply tent as soon as we arrived. Uniforms were issued and we returned to our barracks.

Camp Upton, Long Island, New York

At réveille the next morning, Corporal Benny marched us to our area and we were told we were to clean up the grounds.

Benny lined us up and in his gravelly voice barked, "All youse guys with a high school education take one step forward." Many of us did. "Youse guys with a college education take two steps forward." A handful of us stepped again. "Okay. Youse high school guys pick up all the cigarette butts. Youse college guys pick up all the matches and everything else.

Youse other guys, you stand right there and get a education!"

Many years later I saw this same story recounted by another WWII veteran whose basic training took place somewhere else entirely. I am not sure whether the story became legend—maybe a Reader's Digest humor in uniform anecdote—or many basic training corporals played the same game.

We left Camp Upton for infantry training at Fort McClellan, Alabama. That was a little unfortunate. I mean, infantry basic in Alabama in June, July and August? It was grueling!

Training was very difficult. I was not in good physical shape. A regular teenager, basically. I wasn't really one of these muscular guys. I went in weighing about 165 pounds and I was only 5-foot-8 at most. I think when I was finished I was about 135. Unfortunately, I was still only 5-foot-8.

There was a theater in town, and if we had time off we could go. It was Alabama. All the blacks had to sit upstairs, even the black soldiers, yet there were German POWs who were brought to the theater from a prison camp nearby and they were allowed to sit downstairs. It was disgraceful.

Then a lucky thing happened. The Army chose me to return to college, part of the Army Specialized Training Program (ASTP). They needed engineers, so they selected soldiers who had completed some college and done well on a test. As many of my fellow privates trained for D-Day or the Italy campaign or the invasion of Pacific Islands, I spent the next two semesters at Alabama Polytechnic Institute (now Auburn University).

There I was, taking advanced courses like integral and differential calculus without having had the prerequisite math courses. Fortunately, I'd had a math course for pre-med students at Penn State. It was taught by a Lebanese professor named Sibley, and he took us from algebra all the way through calculus. I didn't really understand the theory, but I could solve the problems.

Somehow, I passed. Then, after two semesters, the Army decided they needed riflemen more than engineers and the program was discontinued. However, there was one more way to stay in school rather than picking up a rifle. The Army needed doctors, so they offered another exam, this time to determine if they'd send you to medical school.

About four hundred men took the test, and there were forty openings. This was one of the first times I ran into anti-Semitism in the Army. After taking the test, everyone was interviewed by this one particular Army major, who would select the forty medical students. When the list was announced, many candidates with very high test scores were not on it. Someone noticed that the high scores skipped were from Jewish soldiers. Not one Jewish man was chosen for medical school.

Our ASTP unit was commanded by a general who had graduated from West Point. He was close to eighty years old; he'd been in World War I, retired, and was reactivated to command this unit far from combat. A group of Jewish students who had been skipped on the list asked for an interview with him. When the situation was pointed out to him, he was furious. He received an additional allocation of eight spots and filled them with the top eight Jewish soldiers—but I was not one of them.

Instead, I was assigned to the 106th Division and sent to Camp Atterbury, near Indianapolis. The rest of the division had been doing intensive battle training, in maneuvers in Tennessee. I was lucky to miss that.

In Indianapolis, I was assigned to a rifle company, Company A. But one morning they called names to step forward, including me, and I was told I was going to radio school. So was Charles Wesley Caldwell. His nickname was Blue, after a hog in the movie State Fair, or so he told me. His brother was nicknamed Brown after another hog in the movie.

Blue was a tall, good-looking gentleman of the old South, from Natchez, Mississippi. He was one of the nicest guys around. We were in the same platoon and became good friends. Little did we know that we'd follow the same path all the way through the war.

In radio school, we learned Morse Code. You had to be able to receive and send 13 words a minute. The messages were all sent in coded words of five letters each. Blue and I were assigned to the communications platoon of the First Battalion of the 423rd Regiment.

On one occasion we got a pass to go into town. This was at Camp Atterbury, near Indianapolis, where the division prepared to go overseas.

There are two ways you could get into Indianapolis: You could take a bus or you could hitchhike. The wait for the bus could be hours.

Blue and I decided to try hitchhiking. We stood there, maybe ten feet apart, with our thumbs up.

A car came along. There were two lieutenants inside, and there was room in the car but they didn't stop. I heard Blue say, "Goddamn Jews." I was shocked. This was my best friend. Either I would break the friendship up or I'd ignore the slur. I chose to ignore it. Our friendship probably saved us both in prison camp.

In the summer of 1944, more than a year after I'd entered the military, orders came for us to pack up and board a troop train. We didn't know where we were going. We scanned the stations we passed and determined we were headed East. As the train continued, we came to New Jersey, and I knew we were going to New York City. The train stayed in Grand Central Station through the night, and the next morning it pulled out, heading toward Long Island. Wouldn't it have been nice if it had been heading for the Hamptons!

Instead, it took a left turn and headed north. Soon I realized that we were going to pass right by my home, which overlooked the station in Larchmont, NY. As we got to Larchmont, we were going slowly enough that I could recognize people on the platform—because of my parents' store, I knew a lot of faces. I felt like jumping off the train, but of course, it wasn't going that slow.

The train continued into Massachusetts, where there was a holding camp for divisions shipping overseas. We had 18,000 men ready to go. After several weeks, we got back on the train, passing though Larchmont again.

We sailed from New York Harbor.

CHAPTER

— FOUR —

We sailed to Europe on the Queen Elizabeth. It was still a new ship: it had been launched in 1938 as one of the premier luxury liners of its day, at a time when all travel from the U.S. to Europe was still by sea. Most soldiers didn't go over on the Queen Elizabeth, but like everything else, the ship had been pressed into service for the troops. The ship was fast enough to outrun a U-boat (though incredibly deadly, the German submarines were quite slow) so it did not need to be part of a convoy. Sailing solo made it harder for the U-boats to spot.

Queen Elizabeth

On the ship, they put the lowest-rank people down in the bowels and worked their way up: the lesser officers would get quarters, then the higher officers, then the commanding officer and his staff in what had been the luxury suites.

Apparently when they got to the top there were two cabins left over. My company was lucky enough to get those two. They had the very few showers onboard that had fresh water. That's what I remember. The beds were in sets of six, starting on the floor and going to the ceiling.

In our room we had 24 men, four groups of six hammocks. The biggest craps game on the trip, I think, was in our room. I also learned how to play blackjack. You had to have the deal. That's when you could make money.

We landed in Scotland at the end of September, 1944, and traveled by train to Cheltenham, England, where we spent the next several weeks. We had arrived, but our heavy equipment had not. A week or two after our arrival, all qualified drivers were ordered to report to Division HQ. I had qualified as a Jeep driver so off I went. Our job was to pick up our equipment in Scotland and bring it back to the camp.

When we got to Edinburgh, we were assigned vehicles on a first come, first served basis. When it was my turn, I was shocked when I was assigned a 2½-ton truck. In training, I had driven this kind of vehicle one time for about ten minutes. The guys in the convoy teased me that after we had driven through downtown Edinburgh there was a trolley car that had no paint on one side (my doing). The route took us on a narrow, two-lane road over a mountain. There was a lot of oncoming traffic. There were no guard rails. It was a harrowing drive.

On my next trip, I was assigned a command car used to transport commissioned officers. We were divided into groups of twenty to thirty vehicles led by an officer in another command car. My car acted like a mother hen to the convoy. My job was to start at the rear of the convoy, pass all the vehicles, report to the commanding officer that all was well, and then drop to the rear and start all over again.

This sounds easier than it was. Coming in the opposite direction on this narrow road were British lorries, some carrying parts of airplanes which had been shot down and were being used for replacement parts. In England, you drive on the wrong side of the road which is difficult enough. But having to pass oversized military vehicles as you travel on the other side of the road against oncoming traffic is hairy.

A couple of weeks later we were on our way to the Continent.

We crossed the England Channel on a small packet ship. Our duffel bags were tied down on deck and the men were packed in below. It was a very rough trip and soon men started to get seasick. I was always a good sailor. In order to avoid the stench, I went up on deck, sat on a pile of duffel bags and watched the sea rise up then fall. It was like being on a thrill ride at an amusement park. And the air was so fresh!

Hours later we arrived at Le Havre, France. After disembarking, we were marched inland to a bivouac area.

We no sooner got settled than an officer approached me. "You're no longer a radio operator," he said. "You've been reassigned to a heavy weapons platoon. You are now an anti-tank cannoneer." "I'm a what? Anti-tank cannoneer? What the f**k is that?"

I soon found out I was one of a team responsible for a 57-millimeter anti-tank gun ('57' for short), essentially a modern (for 1944) portable cannon with a long muzzle. We had a truck to tow it. Stopping German tanks was the first order of business as ground troops engaged in battle. I don't think at the time that I'd ever seen a 57, much less trained on one. In fact, I didn't get to see one until the equipment caught up to us that night. When it arrived, the gun was covered in cosmoline, a very thick grease which protected it in its shipment over the Atlantic.

My first "training" was to get the cosmoline off the gun. It was a miserable job. We used rags soaked in gasoline, which melted the cosmoline. The night was very cold and the evaporating gasoline froze our fingers. One of the men found a metal garbage can cover, poured in some gas and threw in a match. Everyone jumped, but there was no explosion. In fact, the fire gave off quite a bit of heat. We would take turns leaving the gun, walking twenty or thirty steps to the fire, then trying to warm up our gas-covered hands. How we didn't set ourselves on fire I'll never know.

Several days later, we moved out. I got my second lesson on the 57. I learned how we attached it to the truck. We rode across France then through Liege, Belgium, traveling past areas that had been battlefields a few months before and towns that had suffered occupation and war. When the convoy stopped, we were surrounded by local citizens of all ages pushing bouquets of flowers and bottles of wine into our truck. Thanks to the fighting of the division we were going to replace, we were liberators. We hadn't yet shot or been shot at; we hadn't shelled or been shelled. For a brief moment, war didn't seem so bad. A short time later we were on our way again, and, hours later, we reached the Schnee Eifel, on the German side of the ridge that formed the border between Belgium and Germany. The enemy was maybe 300 yards away.

CHAPTER

— FIVE —

It was now early December, 1944. It was very cold, so extremely cold. I was lucky in that I had been issued an overcoat. Lots of guys only had short, lightweight Eisenhower jackets, and trying to stay warm was on everyone's mind. My group got lucky, too. We were assigned a pillbox, a concrete bunker along the Siegfried Line, just across the German border. The Germans had built these fortifications, but they'd been captured by our troops in the fall. Our whole company couldn't fit inside. There were about 20 men assigned to the pillbox.

Soldiers with a 57mm antitank gun

Inside it was nice and warm. Oh, my God. We thought we had hit the jackpot. It wasn't so for the riflemen out in their foxholes facing the Germans, who were perhaps 300 yards away. Our pillbox was 100 yards behind the riflemen, and somewhat safe from gunfire. Not so for the riflemen. There were German patrols coming through at night. Our riflemen knew the position of the American patrols. If the American patrols were on the right, and the riflemen heard noise from the left, they'd take out a grenade, pull the pin and just throw it out and let it explode. "Now you want to come closer? Come on, get closer. We'll throw another." That's what they were doing. They were getting very antsy. It was pretty bad for them.

It was here that I learned my job as a cannoneer. There were three 57's in our regiment, each manned by its own squad. One of the guns was positioned in front of the American riflemen. It could only be reached after dark. The other two guns were in more conventional positions behind the protection of the rifle companies. We had antitank ammunition but it was not very effective. If you came up against a Panzer or a Tiger tank, forget about it. The shell would just bounce off. Even if it exploded when it bounced, it didn't do much harm. The only way you could do a German tank any harm was if you hit the treads. If you knocked a tread off, it was disabled.

We took turns on guard duty. It meant being out of the pillbox at night for two hours and then you'd be off for four. In the middle of the night you would hear all sorts of sounds and you'd swear you saw all sorts of movement. Maybe it was just the cold, we thought, or Belgian locals or our own troops. But it wasn't. We heard the Germans preparing to attack.

We were there for about 10 days. On December 16, 1944, early in the morning, we heard a bombardment. We were not in the target area. Shells were coming over us, going past us. It kept up for quite a while. Orders came back to the cooks, "Make all the food. Get the men up to feed them and do it fast." We had a banquet. We had French toast and pancakes and eggs and everything that they had on hand. We were going into battle.

War historians have examined the events that led to the Battle of the Bulge and the miserable days that lay ahead for me and for thousands of my fellow soldiers. With millions fighting in every kind of climate and terrain—land, sea and air—waging the war was incredibly complex. For example, decisions about the planning and manufacturing of war materials weren't just about whether steel went for tanks or ships. With troops in Europe and the Pacific, how do you use resources of every kind? After D-Day, in June 1944, Allied troops had driven the Germans back so rapidly that it appeared the European war might be over before November. The planners in Washington didn't begin making the winter uniforms and boots that we so desperately needed that December—and in the months that followed.

Then there was the weather. WWII bombers were mostly effective in clear weather, when they could fly high enough to avoid being shot down and still drop bombs with some degree of accuracy—the bombardiers needed clear skies to navigate and to see their targets. The low cloud cover of those weeks eliminated our most valuable weapon.

Our own Army's successes also led to this one big failure. The Allied generals knew there would still be a lot of fighting ahead, but they thought the Germans were in retreat, falling back to desperately defend pre-war German borders. It didn't occur to them that the Germans were capable of—or interested in—mounting a major counterattack.

The shelling we heard was that German counterattack. The Germans had marshaled a large force, some 400,000 men and some of their best tanks and mobile weapons, against our Allied force of about 200,000. To both the north and south of our position, German troops were advancing incredibly quickly—creating the Bulge. That morning, as we ate that breakfast, the 422nd and 423rd regiments were being surrounded.

The shelling went on for three or four hours. Then our officers received orders to break out of the trap forming around us. All the vehicles were lined up into a convoy and we were going to fight our way back to St. Vith, a Belgian town we had passed on our way to the front.

My squad's 57-millimeter anti-tank gun was the only one in our battalion that was still operational. The one positioned beyond the riflemen could not be retrieved. Our second 57 had lost a wheel and it was a goner. The convoy's officers told us, "You are now the rear guard. You're the last truck in the convoy. As soon as the convoy stops, unhitch your gun from the truck and get it ready to fire to the rear. Stay there for 15 to 20 minutes. If you don't see the Germans, load up again, get the hell back on the road and catch up to us. When you get there, unload, set it up, same thing again. Okay?"

That's what we did. We were the last defense between the convoy and any German troops behind us.

It was night when we stopped for the first time. Our 20-pound shells came in canisters. One guy on the truck pulled off the cover of the canister. The next guy put two-sided tape on the shell to make less likely to be dropped and handed it off the truck to me. I handed it to another guy. It went through three of us, to the gun. The sergeant loaded it, ready to fire.

No Germans. We hitched the gun back onto the truck and moved on.

At the next stop we began to pass another shell, but nobody put the tape on it. When I grabbed it, the shell slid out of my cold hands and hit the macadam road. Clang, clang, clang. It was bouncing. Nothing happened. When we started to breathe again, we loaded it up. Nobody said a word. Nobody said, "What the f**k did you do?" We got back in the truck and drove to catch up with the convoy.

Now we were getting to where the battle was going on. We set our gun up near a wrecked armored vehicle. It was a not a tank. It was a fast-moving tank destroyer, with wheels, not treads. This one had been hit and it was ruined. Nobody around. I'm sure there were dead bodies inside. We were looking at this charred wreck and all of a sudden there were flashes all around us like enormous fireflies. The night was pitch black. Fireflies, what the f**k are those? We realized that tank destroyer had been hit with a phosphorous shell, used to create smoke and havoc and to force tank crews to abandon their tanks. The smoke was gone, but the phosphorous was still glowing. It was like a dream. It was terrible. Like a nightmare.

CHAPTER

— SIX —

The convoy disintegrated. Trucks ran out of gas and were abandoned. Others got stuck in ice and mud caused by all the vehicles that had gone before. Some slid off the road. The road became impassable. We had to leave our truck and gun and just walk west toward St. Vith. We were no longer the rear guard cannoneers. We were riflemen on foot like everyone else.

U.S. convoy near St. Vith

Everyone was exhausted now, not having slept for about 48 hours. In spite of the freezing cold, we collapsed to the icy ground. There was little noise and no one was moving or seemed to know what to do. I lost track of my cannon team; among the hundreds of men nearby, I didn't recognize anyone. Soldiers were too tired to dig foxholes. A malaise started to set in. An officer stood up and spoke. I don't remember his exact words, but I remember his meaning: "Men, we are cut off from the American lines. The last we heard we are not going to be reinforced. In fact, we no longer can communicate with division. However, we know that we must fight our way west to St. Vith. Therefore, I am ordering an attack. All right, let's get started. What officer will take the right flank?"

At that point, another officer stood up and said, "I'll take it. Headquarters Company, follow me." Of course, there was no Headquarters Company. There were just random groups of soldiers from all the various companies. But he seemed smart and confident and I decided he was the one I wanted to follow. About 20 other men joined in.

We went along for quite a way, maybe two miles. We could hear explosions in the distance, but there was no fighting where we were.

I was anticipating a firefight and I didn't even have a rifle. Cannoneers were armed with pistols so we could handle the shells without being encumbered by rifles. In training I had been very proficient with the M-1 carbine rifle. On the other hand, I would have been better off with a sling shot rather than a pistol. If I was firing a pistol at you, the safest place to stand would be about ten feet directly in front of me.

As we moved along we saw dead American soldiers, killed just a short time before. During the month of battle, there would be 19,000 Americans killed and almost 80,000 wounded; these were a few of the first. In our state, the horror didn't start to sink in. My thought was to get rid of my damned pistol and get me a real gun. I picked up the carbine of a dead comrade. His face was in a grimace that was almost a smile. He was not going to need his gun—and I might.

We walked in single file. Our little group on the "right flank" could not see the main group of American soldiers to our south but we knew they were there. Action started to pick up. We could hear small arms fire. The forest we were going through must have been planted by Germans: the trees were all nicely lined up. A bullet fired down the row of trees ricocheted off a branch about six inches above my helmet.

We had been on the move for an hour or two when we spied a German combat patrol heading right for us. We hid and they didn't see us, but four of us at the end of the line had to wait for them to pass and were separated from the rest. We started forward, hoping to catch up, but we lost track of the men ahead of us. In one day, we'd gone from a heavily armored Army Division to a "right flank" of 20 men to four soldiers just hoping to survive.

Later in the day we heard a tremendous barrage to our left. Someone was really getting hammered and we concluded it was the main body of our troops. The Germans had what were called tree bursts. A bomb would come in, hit a tree and explode, turning the tree into it shrapnel. Everyone under the tree was in danger. In addition to the exploding armor of the bomb, soldiers were killed or injured by tree branches and splintered limbs. It was devastating.

Daylight was fading. It was now December 18, 1944. It got dark very early. The four of us had to make a plan. "What the hell are we going to do?" I think we were a sergeant, a PFC, and two privates. I never learned the names of the other guys.

Around us were evergreen trees whose branches sprouted about four feet above the ground. Under the weight of the snow the branches had drooped and the ends touched the ground. We had to make a vital decision: try to keep moving or hole up for the night. After a short discussion, we decided to spend the night under one of these tent-like trees.

We now had not eaten since the morning the Germans attacked two days before. In my coat pocket, I found one packet of chocolate powder used to make hot chocolate. We each ate a portion of the powder. We also hadn't slept in days. This night we did try to sleep but it was very difficult. All sorts of noises surrounded us. We heard mortars from one direction. Then we'd hear burp guns from another. We heard what sounded like loud hammering, shouting, and small arms fire. We were cold and we were terrified. Sleep was almost impossible.

As dawn started to break we could see out through the branches. In the dim light, a German soldier approached. He stopped about 15 yards away—and dropped his pants. In the night, they had set up camp and dug a latrine right near our hiding place.

We could have been heroes. We could have killed a couple of Germans with their pants down but we'd be dead. There were probably hundreds of Germans, and four of us.

We turned to the sergeant. He didn't know what the hell to do. Rank suddenly didn't matter. I was a private. I had not gotten a promotion before going overseas because I'd been at school.

I said, "We're going to be killed or captured. The only thing we can do is destroy our guns so they can't use them against our own troops. Bury the ammunition. Get rid of your firing pin."

We came out under a white flag, someone's handkerchief. We looked around. The Germans had moved on. Unbelievable. We started walking up a hill. Then we started running up. We knew there was a road to St. Vith in this direction but didn't know how far it was. Maybe we could sneak through. We approached the top of the hill and somebody yelled, "Halt."

There were four German soldiers. Two of them must have been 15 years old, two of them must have been 60. They had rifles. We had a white flag.

From the top of the hill we were able to look down at the road and there was a parade like 42nd Street on Christmas Day: An endless convoy of German vehicles and tanks going in the direction of Saint Vith. We could never have gotten away.

The Germans marched us to a barn. Inside there were eight or ten other G.I.'s. The guys who were there already were very sullen, quiet, not saying a word. A German officer came through, looking for American officers. The sergeant I'd been captured with stood up and said something to him. The officer stopped and looked at him, then motioned for the sergeant to come outside. A little while later the sergeant came in and he had part of a loaf of bread and something else, it looked like bologna. He didn't share it with anyone. We hadn't eaten in days. Anybody in that barn who had a gun would have killed him, I'm sure. Here he came back with food. What the hell did he tell the Nazis?

CHAPTER

— SEVEN —

They formed us up and we started marching deeper into Germany with hundreds of other American POWs. We were a sorry mess. We had not eaten in days. We were dirty, hungry, miserable and cold.

Mostly we were on country roads. At times, we could look down on a town below us, snow covered, with a church steeple in the middle, as yet untouched by battle. It looked like a Christmas card.

American prisoners walk past a German Tiger tank

In the farmland in Germany, late in the fall, the families would gather the remaining apples on their trees and keep them in cool attics. This allowed them to have apples through the winter. As we passed one farm house, an elderly woman had a large basket of apples which she was handing out to the POWs. I got a small one, mostly dried out, but it tasted better than any steak I've ever eaten. It was the first food of any kind I'd had in days except for that packet of chocolate.

My memory of the two weeks between my capture and my arrival at the prison camp includes vivid recollections of many incidents, but I'm not that clear on how many days we marched, or were on the train, or rode in a truck. Carl Wouters, a local historian who has devoted himself to detailing the Battle of the Bulge, suggests that we were marched about 20 miles to Gerolstein, where the Germans had a working train depot. At one point, six German planes flew over us at a speed that did not seem possible. We later discovered that these were jets, much faster than planes any of us had seen before. Jets were invented too late to make a big difference in the war.

As we were about to enter the city, off in the distance something was shooting almost straight up into the air leaving a plume of smoke behind as it rose. This was our first sighting of V-2 rockets, the long-range missiles that had decimated London. At the time, long-range missiles were incredibly advanced weapons, not part of the U.S. arsenal. In fact, captured German engineers—the same ones who had armed the Nazis— were eventually key to creating the ones we built in the 1950s.

Finally, we reached the railroad. Oh God. You've seen pictures of the Jews jammed into railroad cars? They put probably 120 Jews in a boxcar. They treated us a little better: In my car, there were about 80 of us. They closed us in the train car and locked it. We still hadn't eaten, and there was no food. We had no water. There were no toilets.

There was no chance of lying down. We were all standing until one man had an idea for how we could sit: One man would sit with his legs apart. The next man would sit between his legs and repeat the process. We could all sit down and rest. When almost everyone was seated, it left a small area next to the only opening to the outside, a small barred cutout high in the side of the car.

A steel helmet became the latrine. This for 80 men, many suffering from dysentery. It was terrible. When the helmet was filled, the contents were thrown out the window. Added to all this was the cold. The temperature was below freezing. You just could not get warm. When I blinked my eyes, it felt as if the lids were moving over ice cubes. It was awful!

The train finally pulled out. Now not only did we have no food, but we had no water and that was worse. At least when we were marching we'd been able to scoop up snow for water. Not now.

Early in the morning the train stopped in another wooded area where it not could easily be seen by American pilots flying overhead. Outside was a work detail of Allied prisoners whom the Germans had repairing the railroad tracks. The men closest to the window in our car let the prisoners outside know about our need for water. There was snow, but we had no container to put it in. Finally, "that" steel helmet was passed through the window. The men outside tried to clean it with the icy cold water, then passed it back, partly full of water. Then I found in my pocket a vial of 5 water purification tablets. I had no idea I'd had them. I believe one tablet was enough to purify a gallon of water. The water was passed around and before the train started again each man had a couple of sips of water.

The weather since our capture had been terrible. Snow, ice, fog and bone-chilling cold. But on December 23, according to the New York Times, the sun came out nice and clear. We heard planes and the train stopped. The soldier at the window saw the German guards abandoning the train and taking cover.

Before we could think about it—WHACK!!—a shell came through the car. Everyone dove to the floor. We were lying there three and four deep. There were one or two men on top of me. I felt my hand getting wet. I was able to raise my arm and I realized it was covered with blood. I thought I'd been hit but I felt no pain. Then the man on top of me started to moan that he'd been hit.

At that moment, the door of the boxcar opened and someone yelled, "Everyone out!" We piled out into the open air. There was utter chaos.

We looked up and the sky was crowded with Allied planes. We had been fired upon by our friends, not our enemies. A major started shouting orders and, like a college marching band, the men formed a big "PW". The planes stopped firing at us, but a number of Americans died from friendly fire that day.

Once we were out of the boxcars, we could see what was one of the biggest bombing raids of the war. The terrible weather that had aided the German attack the week before had finally broken, and the Americans were pounding the Germans. We didn't know it then, but the Battle of the Bulge was turning in the Allies' favor. The German air force was being decimated. Troops were racing to the area from other sectors. Ultimately, during the course of the month-long battle, some 600,000 American and 55,000 British troops became involved.

Fighter pilots, who now knew who we were, would fly in low and waggle their wings in recognition. We were in an open area. Bombers were all over the sky. Lead bombers would drop a flare into a target area and minutes later there would be loud distant explosions.

The air was filled with smoke. Some planes were hit by antiaircraft fire and started to disintegrate. We could follow the parts coming down and pray for the sight of parachutes—and we saw many.

I remember the tail of one hit bomber coming down slowly and it started to spin. It was hard to tell where it would land. We hoped it would not be too near us. It had dropped thousands of feet when suddenly a parachute opened. It was the tailgunner.

This went on the whole day, and as daylight faded and the bombing came to an end, somebody called out, "Hey guys, it's Christmas!" Later I would find out that I wasn't the only member of my family who was miserable that Christmas. Back in Larchmont, my parents' store burned to the ground.

When the planes left, the Nazi guards returned. The train was disabled, so we started to march again. We still had several days' march to the prison camp. At the end of one day, many of us were herded into a huge garage to spend the night. Not counting the train, it was the first time we spent the night indoors since the battle started. A German soldier appeared with a large bucket. We were each fed a tablespoon of molasses. It was the first food provided by our captors. We hadn't eaten in about ten days.

The next morning, we were awakened by guards yelling "Rouse, Rouse (Get up)!" and were pushed outside. By this time most of the men had dysentery. Some had frozen feet. Some men just could not get up. An American officer, a big guy with a large handlebar moustache, confronted the guards. He insisted there were many men who could not move. They could never make it to the next destination. He demanded that the Germans provide trucks for the men who were in the poorest condition. German soldiers were very respectful of officers, even American ones. Amazingly, a short time later trucks appeared and many of us were jammed into them.

Many people have asked if I ever suffered atrocities or torture. The answer is nothing except the treatment on the trains and malnutrition at the camp. But an incident at the end of this truck ride underlined the cruelty of some of the guards. When we reached our destination, the tailgate was lowered and we were ordered out of the truck. Men started to ease themselves to the ground. But this was not fast enough for the guards. They started pushing men out of the truck. With frozen feet, the pain on the drop to the ground was excruciating. Maybe not an atrocity, but bad enough to remember after 74 years!

Finally, we arrived at the prison camp, Stalag IV-B. It was New Year's Eve, 1945.

CHAPTER

— EIGHT —

S talag IV-B was near an eastern German town called Muhlberg on the east side of the Elbe River, 300 miles from where we'd first boarded the train. We arrived at about midnight and lined up in front of a barracks. It was snowing and again very cold. That New Year's Eve, we were not celebrating.

When my turn came to enter the building, I saw there were six desks with a line of maybe five men in front of each, waiting to be interrogated. At each desk was an officer in a British uniform. They spoke with English accents. At this point we had been starved, dehydrated, suffered dysentery. I had no expectation of decent treatment. Whether it was from delirium or fear or reasonable suspicion, I was not persuaded by these officers' uniforms or perfect English. It did not make sense to me that I would be registered at a prison camp by British officers. I was sure they were Germans.

As I got nearer to the desks I could hear the questions being asked of the men in front of me. In our training, we had been told that the only information we should supply was name, rank, and serial number. Now the questions were clear:

Name
Rank
Serial number
What was your outfit?
Where were you captured?
Where are you from?
Parents' names?
Religion?

. . . on and on, about thirty questions in all. The men in front of me were answering the questions—and some soldiers I knew were Jewish were lying about their religion. I got angry.

When my turn came, I answered the first three questions, then kept answering "Sorry, Sir. Sorry Sir," as we had been trained. My questioner went through the whole list then stopped and said, in his British accent, "How long has it been since you've eaten, soldier?" This question I answered. "Two weeks, Sir."

"Soldier, I will ask these questions one more time. If you don't answer, you won't eat for another month!"

To not answer now would be suicide, so I answered. When it came to religion, lying seemed the safe thing to do. I hadn't heard anyone else admit to being Jewish. But I didn't care. In my mind I said, "F**k you!" I was young, angry, and by any measure stupid. I answered, "Jewish."

I fully expected to be pulled out of the line by my German interrogator, but I wasn't. I was led out with others and assigned to a barracks. As I remember it, the building was about fifty by eighty feet. The bunks were three-tiered wooden framed and came out three-deep from the wall, which meant that one set of bunks took care of nine men. There were two sets of these bunks and then an aisle, then eighteen more men and another aisle.

There was no mattress or springs, of course. What you had were wooden slats. If you were lucky you had a cloth bag filled with a bit of straw that you put on the cross-pieces. That was your mattress. That would have been okay if you had enough slats. However, previous prisoners had used some of the boards as fuel and so there were gaps that made sleeping extremely uncomfortable. I was issued a thin blanket and, luckily, I had my overcoat.

The next morning guards came through the barracks yelling "Rouse! Arise!" We were lined up and counted. The officer in charge barked out a number of orders in English:

"All medical personnel take one step forward."

"All cooks and bakers take two steps forward."

"All Jews take three steps forward."

Again, I was sure that those of us who identified ourselves as Jewish would be marched off to who knows what fate. We knew the Nazis enslaved and murdered Jews, though we did not then know the extent of the slaughter at the death camps. Along with a number of other Jewish GIs, I stepped forward anyway. We were not rounded up. Some prisoners who had not stepped forward were picked out for work details. The rest of us were dismissed.

Had I been in another prison camp, that moment might have turned out differently. A contingent of Jewish-American GIs and other "troublemakers" were sent from Stalag IX-B to the Berga slave camp, part of the Buchenwald complex. Some were worked to death. More died on a forced march as Allied troops approached.

Over time, I learned how the camp worked, and why Jewish soldiers were not abused. By this point in the war, the Germans had minimized the number of German guards at POW camps to send more soldiers into battle. Most of the guards were not German, but from the countries Germany had annexed. Allied officers, mostly British, were in charge of a lot of the internal workings at the camp. They did their best to protect Jewish soldiers, keeping us from interacting with German guards or civilians. My interrogator had in fact been British, and the comprehensive information he'd demanded allowed him to notify the War Department, the Red Cross, and in turn my parents of my capture. My defiant pronouncement about my religion probably helped save my life.

According to Carl Wouters' historical research, not only did the Allied officers protect us from the Germans, but the Germans themselves did not want Jewish prisoners on work details outside the camp, where we would meet German civilians. They did not want civilians to know that there were brave, strong American Jews, willing to fight. It belied their propaganda.

Stalag IV-B was the largest German prison camp, with 30,000 POWs of all nationalities—33 nations in all. There were more than 7,000 British prisoners, enough that the Welsh and the Scots each had their own camp publications. The Soviets were held in a separate sub-camp, where starvation and disease were the norm. In the first years of the war, three quarters of the Russian POWs there died of malnutrition and typhus. Ironically, after the war, Stalag IV-B became a notorious camp for political prisoners held by the East German/Soviet bloc.

Until the Battle of the Bulge, there were few Americans at Stalag IV-B. We made up for that with an influx of 3,000 POWs. The most famous, the writer Kurt Vonnegut, was transferred to another camp closer to Dresden, the scene (along with Outer Space) of his brutal satirical novel about the war, Slaughterhouse Five.

That first day in camp I discovered what our diet would consist of: a cup of non-descript soup, a chunk of black bread and a small potato or two—maybe 800 calories on a good day. In addition, we would get a cup of ersatz coffee that was barely warm. Some prisoners didn't drink the "coffee" but used the warm liquid to shave. In my four months in the camp, I remember showering only once. While the long-term prisoners had earlier set up recreational sports leagues and published magazines, by this point in the war there wasn't a lot of activity in the camp—it was cold, it was winter, and there wasn't enough food to make running around seem fun.

My best friend in the Army, Blue Caldwell, was in my barracks. His was the first friendly face I'd seen. We got together to try to support each other. We shared our food and tried to do our best to survive. The food was inadequate and it seemed the temperature just kept dropping. The barracks had no heat and was just about as cold as outside. Again, many men had dysentery and just about everyone was as miserable as I.

On the eleventh day in prison camp, I felt I couldn't take much more. I'd heard that you could go on sick call and you would be sent to a barracks that was set up as an infirmary. The important thing was it was heated. If you were lucky, it would take an hour or two before you were examined and for a while you'd be warm. In the States going on sick call when you weren't sick was called "goldbricking." I didn't know if I was sick or not, but I didn't care. I just wanted to get warm.

When I got to the infirmary, it was true: It was warm. I tried to position myself so as not to be taken early. When my turn came, an orderly led me to a doctor. His examination table was a stretcher balanced between two chairs. I sat on it, still savoring the warmth.

As he examined me, he dictated to his orderly. Although some of the words he spoke were English, there was much I could not understand. He was South African, and he was speaking Boer, a combination of Dutch and indigenous African languages. At one point in his dictating he said "TBC." With that, they wrapped me in a blanket and two orderlies carried me off on the stretcher. I knew "TBC" was tuberculosis. The next thing I knew I was in the "Krieg Gefangenen Lazarett" (Prisoner of War Hospital). Now I could admit to myself that I really was sick.

Someone helped me remove my clothes and put on a hospital gown. I got in bed and they put my filthy clothes under my pillow. It was an actual bed and an actual pillow. For that I was grateful.

I shared the ward with about fifteen other men. As I lay there, an ambulatory patient came to my bed, reached under my pillow, and took my clothes. I thought, "This is the end. I'm in a prison camp. I have tuberculosis. Now my clothes have been stolen and I am too weak to do anything about it."

Several hours later this same patient returned. He had cleaned my clothes and folded them neatly. He put them under my pillow. This was my introduction to one of the best people I ever met, my Dutch friend, Ben ter Beek.

The first several days in the hospital I was too weak to get out of bed. Ben took on the job of being my caregiver. When food was delivered to the ward he fed me. As starved as I was, I had no appetite. He would almost force me to have my cup of soup and when I could eat no more, I noticed he would take any uneaten bread and eat it himself. I was sure that's why he was being so nice and taking care of me.

At night, Ben brought a bottle to my bed because I was too weak to get up for the bathroom. Several times each night, he emptied the bottle. There was nothing he gained from that, I can assure you. As I found out, he just did it because it was the right thing to do.

Another doctor determined I didn't have "TBC" but pneumonia. He gave me some pills to take. I believe they were some sort of Sulphur derivative, and they were huge. Some patients had so much trouble swallowing these pills they just hid them. I took every one I was given. I was determined to get better.

As the days wore on I started to improve and my appetite returned. Now when they brought the hospital food, which was a bit better than the food in the camp, I didn't eat it, I devoured it!

Then I noticed something. When my food came, I'd find an extra slice of bread on my plate. Ben was paying me back.

Life in the hospital was better than in the camp. First of all, it was warm—the only heated building I would be in for 6 months. The food was better and we also got special parcels from the American Red Cross when they were available. In the hospital, they were what we called milk parcels, which were designed for sick patients. They contained things like powdered milk and eggs, dried cereal, cheese, and other light foods. One thing in the parcels that I thought were useless were cans of wheat germ. I stored the cans under my bed.

A few days after I entered the hospital another American, Sergeant Joe Prinzinger from Philadelphia, was assigned to my ward. When the Red Cross parcels were distributed, one parcel would be issued to anywhere from two to four prisoners. Joe and I "mucked in" together, which was the British term for sharing our food. He didn't like wheat germ, either, and those cans began to pile up.

The people in the ward came from a number of countries. There were several Greeks. Ben was Dutch. There were three Danes. That was strange, as Denmark had no army. The Danes were not soldiers but policemen. When the Germans invaded Denmark, they took prisoner the only uniformed group who could give them trouble: the police.

These Danish prisoners were only about three or four hundred miles from home. The Danish Red Cross had little trouble delivering their parcels, and in addition they could receive packages from their families. To us, these Danes were living the life of Riley. They didn't share, though. They would only trade.

About two weeks after I entered the hospital, I was well enough to be up and around. By this time five or six cans of the infamous wheat germ were under my bed. One day, Ben gathered up all the cans and disappeared. I knew that Ben, who had been a prisoner for more than three years, knew his way around and could do things we could not, like trade with the Germans. But what happened next still brings tears to my eyes. Ben appeared several hours later. Somehow, he had traded some of the wheat germ for the necessary ingredients and had baked a cake. He was able to make frosting and on top had spelled out:

CHEERS FOR USA

It was probably the heaviest cake—and the most delicious one—I have ever eaten. The whole ward gathered around to gape. We gave pieces to the other patients, but not to those Danish policemen.

In prisoner of war camps, each nationality had a representative known as a "Man of Confidence." If a problem arose, this person would deal with the British officers or the German commandant. There had been so few Americans before December 1944 that we had no American Man of Confidence in the hospital. We Americans chose the Dutch Man of Confidence to represent us. His name was Danny and he was a wonderful person.

Danny liked to play bridge. He found out that Joe Prinzinger and I could play, and one late afternoon he came into the ward with a South African doctor and we started to play bridge. Time slipped by, and it got dark outside. The orderlies whose job it was to announce "lights out" came by. We were in the middle of a rubber and Danny wanted to finish. He told the orderlies that as the Man of Confidence he was in charge, and we went on playing. They went berserk, but the more they jabbered at us the less attention we paid to them.

Twenty minutes later, we finished our game. Danny stood up and said "Thanks for the game—lights out."

My hospital stay ended about four weeks after I had entered. Joe and I were marched back to the camp and assigned to the same barracks. I was delighted that Blue was there as well. The three of us got together with a fourth American GI, Jimmy McCormick. Jimmy had been in the 1st Infantry Division. He had been through the African Campaign but I think he was captured in Italy.

The four of us mucked in together, sharing food and supporting each other. If Red Cross parcels arrived, sometimes eight prisoners would have to share one parcel. Unlike the hospital parcels, these had things like a can of tuna or salmon or spam. But the most important thing in the parcel was a carton of two hundred American cigarettes—Lucky Strikes, Chesterfield, Camels. These cigarettes were the currency of Stalag IV-B.

Distributing free cigarettes to American soldiers had begun in WWI and was a major part of rations during WWII. I don't know if the cigarette companies knew then that cigarettes were addictive, but cigarette smoking became much more common when it became part of every soldier's life. I was one of the few who did not smoke, but I knew every cigarette's value in trade.

The way we split up the parcels was something that I used later in my career as an accountant. If there were eight of us to share one parcel, one person would divide it into eight separate piles. Each of us chose one portion, with the person who had split up the parcel choosing last. That person was very careful to divide things as equally as possible because he was going to get the worst. The next time the Red Cross parcel came through, the guy who had been last became first and everyone dropped down a notch.

In subsequent years, after I became an accountant, I might be advising clients, business partners who decided to part ways. I always suggested that one partner divide the assets into two "piles" and the other got first choice. Or, if each partner wanted to buy out the other, one would set the price and the other could choose to either buy or sell. The one setting the price was very careful to set a price that was fair because he didn't know if he was buying or selling.

The Germans had rules for the prisoners, but we prisoners had our own rules, too. The primary rule was that you could steal from the Germans, but you were absolutely never to steal from a fellow prisoner. The reason was simple. Everyone was semi-starved. To steal food was a great temptation, but if you got caught it was as if you'd committed murder. The punishment could kill you.

An American sergeant from my outfit was caught stealing from a fellow prisoner. This sergeant was the model soldier. He could out-march almost any other man. He was good on the firing range. He could take orders and give them equally as well. Apparently one thing he couldn't do well was starve.

When he was caught, a kangaroo court was held in the barracks that night. He was found guilty. The sentence allowed anyone in the barracks to hit, kick or beat the prisoner at will.

There were about two hundred fifty men in our barracks, and in a group that large, you'll always find some sadistically inclined people.

The sergeant received an unmerciful beating, eventually collapsing to the floor. Several prisoners dragged him outside and left him in the area between our barracks and the next one. It was midwinter. Somehow, he survived. I am not aware of any other prisoner in our barracks stealing again.

I was never sent on a work detail, such as working on a farm or in a mine. I attributed that to the British officers who were running the camp and protecting Jewish prisoners. But one day I was one of about twelve prisoners assigned to pick up a load of food—potatoes and turnips. This was a coveted opportunity to trade cigarettes for food with the civilians. The only problem was that if the German guards found out, they would confiscate whatever you had.

Our group pushed and pulled a large wagon which ordinarily would have had a horse doing the work. We left the camp under guard and were led to the earthen mounds where the potatoes and turnips were buried.

Another group there loaded the wagon. There were several civilians present and this is where the trading could take place.

Jimmy McCormick had a paratrooper's jumpsuit which was very loose fitting and had lots of pockets. It buttoned about eight inches below the crotch. There were pockets on the outside and the inside of the jacket and some on the inside and outside of the legs. This is what I wore leaving camp.

For eight cigarettes I was able to buy a big loaf of black bread. I hid it in the pocket between my legs.

When the wagon was filled, we had to push it back to camp. Of course, this was much tougher than the trip out because it was now weighed down with potatoes.

At the camp gate, the guards searched the wagon, looking under the wagon itself and then digging through the load. They found nothing. I tried to stay as inconspicuous as possible and fortunately I was not searched.

As we left the gate, we headed for the prison kitchen. A prisoner ran up to the wagon, grabbed a turnip and ran. Our guard shouted to him to halt but he kept on running. The guard aimed his rifle and fired. I never knew if the prisoner was hit.

I sometimes wonder if I dreamt some of the things I remember from Stalag IV-B. There was one barracks where prisoners would set up maps of Europe and track the progress of the Allied troops. On the maps they would mark the advances of the Allied armies from the west and the Russian army's advances from the east. At one point the Russians advanced as close as sixty miles from our camp and then stopped. We waited days for them to advance. Though much further away, the American, British, French and others kept moving forward. Our hero and hope was General George Patton, who led a mechanized force which was advancing faster than anyone else.

The mystery to me is how we got those detailed reports. The Germans were mystified, too. They searched many barracks looking for the radio. They never found it. My guess is that a number of POWs carried parts of a radio with them, came together at a specific time each day, assembled the radio, got the news and then disassembled the radio and disappeared. To the best of my knowledge the Germans never found anything.

As the weather improved, Joe Prinzinger made the rest of us get out and walk. He made sure we didn't just waste away. Even in our state, exercise was important. One day as we passed a barracks occupied by French POWs, we were stunned by a delicious aroma. As we walked closer we saw that several men had built a small fire and were cooking a big pot full of peas and what looked like pigeons. Where they got the food, I don't know. There wasn't a chance that they were going to share any of that meal, so we just walked on—and dreamed.

If Joe kept us fit, Jimmy McCormick kept us upbeat. He was a very positive guy. I still remember the songs he sang.

There was a book that was being passed around, one of the few books in the camp, and everyone got a turn. It was ironic: the title of the book was Ordeal by Hunger, and it was about the Donner Party, the pioneers who turned to cannibalism. Everyone looked at you very suspiciously while you were reading it.

The fighting was getting closer and we would see planes come over and hear the bombings. We heard when they bombed Dresden in February, and we could see the glow from the burning city at night. We were cheering them. On one of the bombing runs in March, a plane inadvertently shot into our camp. One of the shells went through our barracks. Fortunately, it didn't hit anybody. This was within a month of being liberated. We could have died from friendly fire.

The first day of Passover in 1945 was March 29. Joe Sedaka, a Sephardic Jew I'd known very slightly during training, came by my barracks. He said, "Come with me." I said, "Where are we going?" He said, "Never mind. Just come with me." I said, "Okay," and followed him. We got near a barracks and looked to make sure no guards were watching. We didn't want anyone to be aware that a group was assembling.

When we went inside, there was a group of Jewish soldiers celebrating Passover. Not a Seder—we didn't have the food—but a Passover service. There were probably 15 soldiers there. We went through the whole thing under the nose of the Nazis. Joe had a lucky charm in his wallet that his grandfather had given him at a Seder before Joe left for the Army: It was a small piece of matzo wrapped up in a cloth. For our Passover, we were able to bless a real piece of matzo.

On April 12, 1945, President Roosevelt died, and we found out pretty quickly. We had a memorial service for Roosevelt in the camp. The guards just stood by. They knew the end was coming. They didn't interfere.

Finally, on April 23, a Russian officer rode into camp—I'm not exaggerating—on a white horse. He had weapons coming out of his boots: a submachine gun and a rifle and everything else. He was armed to the teeth. He came into the camp and said, "You're free. You can leave." Not in English, in Russian. Somebody understood.

Here we were, free. The first thing we wanted to do was get some food. We didn't care what kind of food it was. Blue, Joe, Jimmy and I left the camp, went to the mounds where the Germans stored the potatoes, and brought a bunch of them back to the camp. We got some wood and baked the potatoes. The four of us sat there eating potatoes on the night we were liberated.

I reached into my pocket and pulled out four cigarettes, real Lucky Strikes. Those were considered the best because the advertising campaign said they were "fully packed." We celebrated our freedom and the Allied victory over Germany by eating potatoes and smoking cigarettes without breaking them to make them last longer. Even I, who did not smoke, had a few puffs. We felt so lucky.

CHAPTER

— NINE —

The next day the guards were gone, but we didn't immediately leave the camp. The war was not over. There was still firing going on, and the camp seemed like the safest place to be. After a day or two—I don't remember exactly—a group of us left the camp, heading for the town of Riesa, about 10 miles south of Stalag IV-B. The Russians had set up a facility there for freed POWs.

Along the way, we found an abandoned house. It had to have been left by a Nazi official because there were very expensive things in the house. I remember a silver wine cooler. The cover was a big swastika. A lot of soldiers were taking items—one had rolled up a tapestry—but I couldn't have carried that one.

When we went into the basement, there were piles of American Red Cross parcels that had been meant for the prisoners. But we didn't have to open them for food. Out back, there were rabbits and a chicken. Skinning rabbits and beheading chickens wasn't an expertise I'd acquired in Larchmont, but my compatriots knew what to do. We had rabbit stew.

My friend Norman found a barrel of flour. He said, "You know, I know how to make a challah." He went through the whole process of mixing it up and baking it. But it turned out it wasn't flour he'd found—it was plaster of Paris.

In Riesa, we were housed in four buildings in a quadrangle like college dorms. We really didn't know what was going to happen—how long we'd be there or how we were going to be transferred to the American lines.

The Russians gave us what was called a "short arm" inspection to make sure no one had venereal disease. I'd had those inspections before, but this was new: the Russian doctor was a woman.

At one point, an American Major in a Jeep pulled into the quadrangle. He was trying to negotiate getting us back to the U.S. lines. At the top of his voice, he said, "I have trucks here on the road, and I'd like to take our prisoners back." The Russians said no, they wanted to release us when the Americans brought back Russian prisoners. There was a wariness between the two Allies.

While we were in the Russian facility, the Germans surrendered, and the European war was declared over. It was May 8, 1945, two weeks after Stalag IV-B had been liberated. The Russian soldiers went crazy, dancing and firing their guns. We were worried—bullets that go up come down, too.

The American POWs were waiting for some kind of orders to return to American lines, but the Russians didn't guard us or require us to stay in Riesa after that. The day after the Germans surrendered, a group of us left and started walking west toward the Mulde River, where the American troops had stopped, about 25 miles away. No one stopped us.

We hitched a ride with a couple of drunk Russian soldiers in a horse and wagon. At one point, we passed a high hedge. One of the Russians heard something; he drew a gun and started firing at the hedge, but high. A bunch of children ran out. They could have been killed for no reason.

The next day, we stopped at a farm. The family living there was terrified of us. We weren't going to hurt them, but we did want to eat and a place to stay. They had eggs, and we hadn't had fresh eggs in a long time.

One of the guys said he wanted some fried eggs. He was trying to describe to the German woman how he wanted them made. The woman went out and got all the eggs there were, but instead of putting them in the frying pan she baked them. No fried eggs.

We stayed overnight at the farm. I had my own room with a feather bed and clean sheets, all to myself—and a radio. I turned on the radio and I was able to get the Armed Forces Network. I listened to a musical show, and Cass Daley, a popular singer of the time, was singing.

I ran out and told the guys to come in because they're singing a song about us. They ran in. The song was "Don't Fence Me In."

It took three or four days to reach the Mulde from Riesa. When we got to the river, there was a bridge that had been bombed out, but you could still walk across it. We just had to cross and we were in American territory.

I try to remember how I felt right then, crossing to safety, but I don't have a clear memory. We were too tired and weak to feel exultant or free.

American soldiers welcomed us—but wouldn't touch us. We were filthy and potentially infested. They had us strip and hosed us down, probably with DDT. DDT was used extensively—and successfully—during WWII to prevent the spread of typhus in Europe and malaria in the Pacific.

They got us clothes and put us in rooms in an abandoned hotel. Best of all, there was food. They did their best to get us whatever we wanted. I remember asking for a steak—and getting one.

We were there for a couple of days, then we went to an airfield to wait for a plane to take us to Camp Lucky Strike in France. The camps where they brought the ex-POWs before sending us back to the States were all named after cigarette brands, of course—more good marketing. At the airfield, there were groups of different nationalities waiting to be flown home. I remember 105 American planes came in—I was overwhelmed with emotion when I saw them. Each one could carry about 25-30 prisoners. Allied soldiers from the other countries were still waiting. Their planes hadn't come in, and we felt so sorry for them.

That was my first flight. The planes were made for paratroopers. The seats had no backs so there was room for a parachute.

I was on the plane with Blue. We sat there amid crates of food: C-rations, not K-rations. K-rations fed you for a day if you were in combat. These were cans of franks and beans and spaghetti and meatballs, and beef stew. We were all crazy for food. One of the guys broke open a crate, took out what he wanted, and started to build a fire with the wood from the crate.

We were watching him, basically dazed. This guy was going to cook his franks and beans over a fire on the floor of an airplane. One of the crew, an officer, came out and put a stop to it.

CHAPTER

— TEN —

Camp Lucky Strike, one of several large transition camps for ex-POWs, was north of Le Havre, France, near the coastal town of Saint-Valery-en-Caux. We got to the camp and it seemed like nobody was being sent home. We thought there were no transport ships available. Looking back on it I think that they were keeping us there to fatten us up while they shipped home troops that were in better shape. The ex-POWs were emaciated. At Lucky Strike, you could have food any time you desired—cheese sandwiches (which Jimmy McCormick must have loved), milkshakes… Nothing ever seemed like such a luxury.

The Army had set up an outdoor theater. One evening, Blue suggested we go to see the movie, Gaslight, with Charles Boyer and Ingrid Bergman.

On the way, he said, "Milt, there's something that's been bothering me for a long time." I knew what it was. He apologized for the day at Camp Atterbury when he'd used an anti-Semitic epithet. He told me he'd written to his father and asked for his advice about what to do. His father was a wise man: he wrote, "Blue, just be a good friend." And that he certainly was—and remained.

He apologized, but I had forgiven him long before. If he had never apologized, it wouldn't have mattered.

In later years, I reconnected with Blue. On our annual trips to California, my wife Shirley and I stopped in Mississippi to spend a day with him and his family on our way to California. One visit, he pulled out a copy of the local newspaper to show me a big story about him. In the article, he credited me, a Jewish soldier from New York, with saving his life. I felt he'd saved mine. We were both right.

General Eisenhower came through Camp Lucky Strike, reviewing the troops. He passed within about 10 feet of me, shaking hands with the nearest men. He came to one guy who looked very disheveled, and he said, very kindly, "Young man, don't you think you'd feel better if you shaved?" He was a mensch.

Frustrated about not getting to go home, one day we all went AWOL (absent without official leave). Everybody was leaving camp. Blue and I started to walk toward one of the bigger towns. But before we got to a town, we walked past a church where a group of French townspeople were celebrating the end of the war. They called us to come in and celebrate with them. They were pouring us Calvados. It's one of the two or three times in my life that I got drunk. I mean, seriously drunk.

While we were there, the American news service started broadcasting: "Will the former prisoners of war please come back to Lucky Strike. There's transportation home waiting for you." There was no transportation. They just wanted to get us back to Lucky Strike.

While we were waiting for the transport ships, planes came into the airstrip. They were continuing on to the Riviera. The camp officials told us that anyone who wanted to could fly to the Riviera, spend a week or two there and then come back and go home. But I didn't want to take the chance that transport ships would come to La Havre while I was gone. Later, I kicked myself for passing up that trip to the Riviera—if I'd gone, I would not have gotten home any later.

CHAPTER

— ELEVEN —

Finally, we sailed for home. When we landed, they took us to Camp Patrick Henry in Virginia. We were able to make telephone calls—if you waited in line behind 50 other guys. I called Shirley at Penn State on graduation day. Her sorority sisters got the call and they ran to get Shirley. She was in line to receive her diploma, but she stepped out of line and ran to the phone. We had little time to talk, but at least she knew I was home.

I also called home. My parents had received telegrams from the Army, first telling them that I was missing, and then telling them I was a POW, but they really didn't know much about where I was or what I was going through. While I was at the POW camp, once a month they would give you a postcard to write to your family. Most of them didn't get through. In my time there, only two got through, and they didn't come in the right order. In the post card my parents received first, I apparently wrote, "I'm okay now," which made them worry about how I'd been earlier— probably when I'd been in the hospital. Many years later, my son, Bob, had the telegrams framed with my medals and they hang on my wall, now yellow and faded.

As happy as they were that I was safe, my parents had bad news for me: my Uncle Benny had died in May, after the combat had ended—it was some kind of accident. They told me he had heard about my release from prison camp and was trying to locate me when he died.

So, after the war had ended, my grandmother became a Gold Star mother. My other uncles and I had all made it through.

Whether in accidents like Uncle Benny's, or from illness, infection, drowning, starvation, and, of course, guns and shrapnel and bombs, more than 400,000 American soldiers died and more than 600,000 were wounded during the war. That barely compared to the tens of millions lost by the Russians, British, Canadians and the other Allies, the six million Jews killed in the concentration camps, and the millions of enemy soldiers and civilians killed, injured, and displaced. It's hard for anyone who didn't live through those years to fathom the amount of death and destruction.

I stayed at camp Patrick Henry for a week or two. They were sending people home on long furloughs while they prepared the paperwork to muster us out of the service. I was furloughed for 81 days, time enough for Shirley and me to get married.

My in-laws arranged the wedding at the Delmonico Hotel in midtown Manhattan. It was a very fancy wedding, with about 100 guests. My parents bought me a summer uniform for the wedding—it was an officer's uniform, but I wore it anyway. Our wedding pictures are very dim; there were no flash bulbs available.

One of our favorite wedding gifts came from Blue Caldwell. It was just a candy dish, but, of course, it was blue. It was very moving.

When my furlough was up, instead of sending me back to an Army camp, they sent me to a resort, The Lake Placid Club—a place that Jews could not have gone before the war. If you were married, you could bring your wife but you had to pay for her. I thought, "How am I going to pay?" But it turned out they only charged a dollar a day for wives. It was the first time in my life I went horseback riding, and the first time I was ever in a motor boat. We were there for three weeks. Then they sent me to Camp Edwards on Cape Cod.

I was able to bring Shirley up to Buzzard's Bay. We had a room in a private home and I could leave the base to spend time with her.

An incident from those weeks shows just how affected I'd been by my imprisonment. I was given a job distributing supplies to the mess halls. I had a truck and three German prisoners of war to help, and we were going to the Officers' Club to deliver toilet paper. I didn't know how to say toilet paper in German, so I pointed to the boxes and said, "Scheisse Papier." The German prisoners started to laugh at my invented slang. Remember, I was just out of prison camp. I was not going to be laughed at by Germans. I pulled out my carbine. They stopped laughing.

I sometimes look back I think to myself, "Would I ever have shot them?" I don't think so. I couldn't have done that. But it says something that I was so volatile, it seemed like an option.

Another time, one of the cooks at the Officers' Club told me they had extra lobsters and offered me some. I brought them home, and Shirley said, "What are we going to do with lobsters?" I had no idea—neither of us had been raised eating shellfish of any kind. I ended up giving them to our landlady. About a week later, she brought us a whole Sunday dinner to eat in our room.

They released me from the Army in October, 1945. Penn State had admitted me to return in February, 1946. Shirley's father worked for a clothing company, Crawford Clothes, and he got me a job there for the months before school started. That was really the first business I'd seen besides the candy store—it helped me decide to go into accounting.

It was funny being back at Penn State after the Army and Stalag IV-B— but it was wonderful. Shirley and I were now older and married, so we became the chaperones at dances at my old fraternity. I had five semesters to finish. Shirley got a Master's in sociology. We got our degrees at the same time and started our life together.

CHAPTER

— TWELVE —

When you're 94, healthy, possessing all your faculties, and able to write the story of your life during a war that took place 75 years ago, you know you've been lucky. As our generation dwindles, interest in WWII veterans has been rekindled, and I'm asked about it, thanked, celebrated and congratulated at every turn. I never thought I was a hero, and do not think so now. But to many, even survival is a form of heroism. So is living to 94.

When I tell my story, I sometimes choke up at the memory of being frozen and starved, or when I think about my parents and the two cryptic telegrams they received—it's still that alive for me. I don't pretend it was easy. But I know that I was lucky in ways large and small. I was lucky to have been sent to school through part of the war, missing many months of battle. I was lucky to meet Blue Caldwell, lucky to have been issued an overcoat, lucky to have avoided the shells and bombs and bullets, lucky to have contracted pneumonia and not tuberculosis. I came back alive and healthy and mentally stable. I came back to Shirley and our children and a successful career, to my grandson, Aaron, and now his son, Elliot.

Shirley died in 2006, and I thought my life would be half empty from then on. But a couple of years later, I got lucky again. I met Renée Bauer, and we've had the kind of late life together that everyone dreams of and, frankly, no one deserves. Every day, we laugh and sing and tell stories. She has encouraged me to tell this one as often and in as many forums as I can.

But every day we also read the papers and watch the news. We see a tug of war: on one side, American citizens who, astonishingly, seem bent on pulling us toward becoming the kind of brutalist, prejudiced society we went to war against in 1941; and on the other side, caring, optimistic (often young) Americans who want to end the stereotypes and propaganda and belligerence on which wars depend.

The war led to tremendous social and global changes, from the end of Jim Crow to the creation of modern Europe and Japan. The women's movement was built in part by women who'd become workers and business professionals while men were overseas. By and large, American soldiers set an example for the world: We won without resorting to torture or rape or subjugation, then, with the Marshall Plan, showed that the U.S. valued functioning societies over national punishment. The global admiration for democracy, and for the United States, soared in the decades after the war.

The America I love and risked my life for is one where Blue Caldwell and I could recognize each other as friends and not stereotypes, where we could have each other's backs through every kind of adversity. It's one where immigrants like my parents can make a life they could not have hoped for in their native country. It's a country built on laws and morality, where we recognize right and wrong, that ends don't always justify means. It's one for which people from countries all over the world might, like my Dutch friend Ben ter Beek, consider risking their freedom to bake a cake that says, "CHEERS FOR USA!"

—**Milton Feldman, with Seth Bauer**
May 4, 2018

ACKNOWLEDGEMENTS

I would be remiss if I did not take advantage of this opportunity to give thanks and credit to my wife's son, Seth Bauer—whom I now consider my son—for creating this book from my writings and my many hours of storytelling. Without his experience as a writer and editor this book would not exist. Credit is also due to my wife, Renée, and my son, Bob Feldman, for encouraging me to bring this to fruition. It takes many helping hands to create a project like this. Thanks go to Joe Fierst for the book design and Roberta Bauer for copy editing. Aaron Feldman, Paul Lucas, Linda Bauer, and Eduardo Montes-Bradley all contributed. And Kevin and Kate Kelly have been instrumental in encouraging Stoneridge Creek veterans to share our stories.

Made in the USA
Middletown, DE
17 September 2018